THE CONSTITUTIONAL CONVENTION

BY BEATRICE HARRIS

Gareth Stevens
PUBLISHING

CRASHCOURSE

Please visit our website, www.garethstevens.com. For a free color catalog of all our high-quality books, call toll free 1-800-542-2595 or fax 1-877-542-2596.

Library of Congress Cataloging-in-Publication Data
Names: Harris, Beatrice, 1978- author.
Title: The Constitutional Convention / Beatrice Harris.
Description: New York : Gareth Stevens Publishing, [2022] | Series: A look at U.S. history | Includes index.
Identifiers: LCCN 2020025925 (print) | LCCN 2020025926 (ebook) | ISBN 9781538266397 (library binding) | ISBN 9781538266373 (paperback) | ISBN 9781538266380 (set) | ISBN 9781538266403 (ebook)
Subjects: LCSH: United States. Constitutional Convention (1787) | Constitutional history--United States.
Classification: LCC KF4510 .H37 2022 (print) | LCC KF4510 (ebook) | DDC 342.7302/42--dc23
LC record available at https://lccn.loc.gov/2020025925
LC ebook record available at https://lccn.loc.gov/2020025926

First Edition

Published in 2022 by
Gareth Stevens Publishing
111 East 14th Street, Suite 349
New York, NY 10003

Editor: Therese Shea

Photo credits: Series art Christophe BOISSON/Shutterstock.com; (feather quill) Galushko Sergey/Shutterstock.com; (parchment) mollicart-design/Shutterstock.com; cover, pp. 1 courtesy of the Architect of the Capitol; pp. 5 (top), 25, 27 (bottom), 29 courtesy of the National Archives and Records Administration; p. 5 (bottom) Stock Montage/Getty Images; p. 7 Bettmann/Getty Images; p. 9 MPI/Getty Images; p. 11 (top) VCG Wilson/Corbis via Getty Images; p. 11 (bottom) Garen Meguerian/Moment/Getty Images; p. 13 JPL Designs/ Shutterstock.com; pp. 15, 23, 27 (top) DeAgostini/Getty Images; p. 17 Visions Of Our Land/ Photolibrary / Getty Images Plus; p. 19 (top) Universal History Archive/Universal Images Group via Getty Images; p. 19 (bottom) Caroline Purser/ The Image Bank/Getty Images; p. 21 Danita Delimont/ Gallo Images / Getty Images Plus.

Printed in the United States of America

Some of the images in this book illustrate individuals who are models. The depictions do not imply actual situations or events.

CPSIA compliance information: Batch #CSGS22: For further information contact Gareth Stevens, New York, New York at 1-800-542-2595.

Find us on

CONTENTS

Words in the glossary appear in **bold** type the first time they are used in the text.

After the **American Revolution**, the United States was free from Great Britain's rule. Starting a new nation wasn't an easy job. The first plan for the government was in the first U.S. constitution. This was called the Articles of Confederation.

ARTICLES OF CONFEDERATION

MAKE THE GRADE

A constitution is a document, or piece of writing, that explains the main laws of a country.

The Articles of Confederation set up the new country as a **"league** of friendship" among states. It didn't give much power to the national government. For example, the government had no power to collect taxes. Still, it owed other countries a lot of money.

MAKE THE GRADE

In 1786, poor farmers in Massachusetts began the Shays's **Rebellion**. Some thought it was a sign a stronger national government was needed.

7

THE ANNAPOLIS CONVENTION

In 1786, **delegates** from five states met in Annapolis, Maryland. They talked about how **interstate** business should work. The **convention** decided the Articles of Confederation needed to be amended, or changed. To do this, another convention in Philadelphia, Pennsylvania, was planned in 1787.

The Annapolis Convention took place at the Maryland State House, shown above. All 12 delegates agreed that the Articles of Confederation needed to be amended.

9

ANOTHER CONVENTION BEGINS

On May 25, 1787, the Constitutional Convention began. Delegates from every state except Rhode Island took part. The delegates decided to write a new constitution rather than amend the Articles of Confederation. Virginia delegate George Washington was chosen to be the convention president.

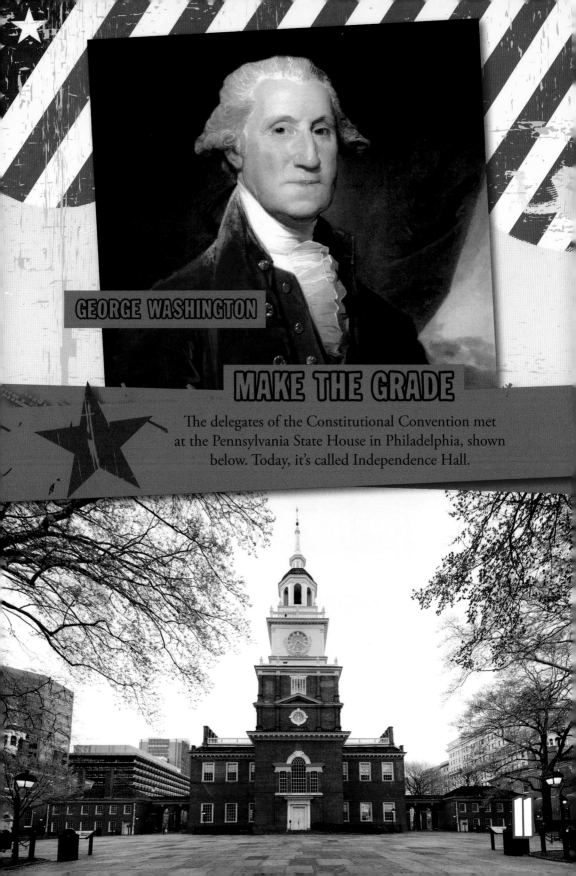

GEORGE WASHINGTON

MAKE THE GRADE

The delegates of the Constitutional Convention met at the Pennsylvania State House in Philadelphia, shown below. Today, it's called Independence Hall.

THREE BRANCHES OF GOVERNMENT

The delegates mostly agreed with Virginia delegate James Madison's plan for a federal, or national, government. The government would be made up of three branches. These are the legislative, executive, and judicial branches. Each has equally important but different powers.

MAKE THE GRADE

The Constitution set up a system of checks
and balances to make sure that no branch
of government became too powerful.

LEGISLATIVE (CONGRESS)

makes the laws

EXECUTIVE (HEADED BY THE PRESIDENT)

carries out the laws

JUDICIAL (FEDERAL COURTS)

explains what laws mean

13

THE LEGISLATIVE BRANCH

Delegates at the Constitutional Convention talked about how many **representatives** each state would have in the legislative, or lawmaking, branch. States with many people wanted more representatives. Small states thought all states should have an equal number of representatives.

MAKE THE GRADE

Southern states had many **enslaved** people at the time of the convention. They wanted to count them to get more representation in the legislative branch.

15

The delegates **compromised**.
Congress has two parts: the Senate
and the House of Representatives.
Each state sends two senators to
the Senate. A state's **population**
decides the state's number
of representatives in the
House of Representatives.

MAKE THE GRADE

The delegates also settled on what's called the three-fifths compromise. Three-fifths of the number of enslaved people would be included in a state's total population.

U.S. CAPITOL, WHERE CONGRESS MEETS

THE EXECUTIVE BRANCH

The delegates decided a leader called the president would head the executive branch. Some wanted the president to serve for life. Others thought that would make the president like a king. So, the president is elected for a four-year period, or term.

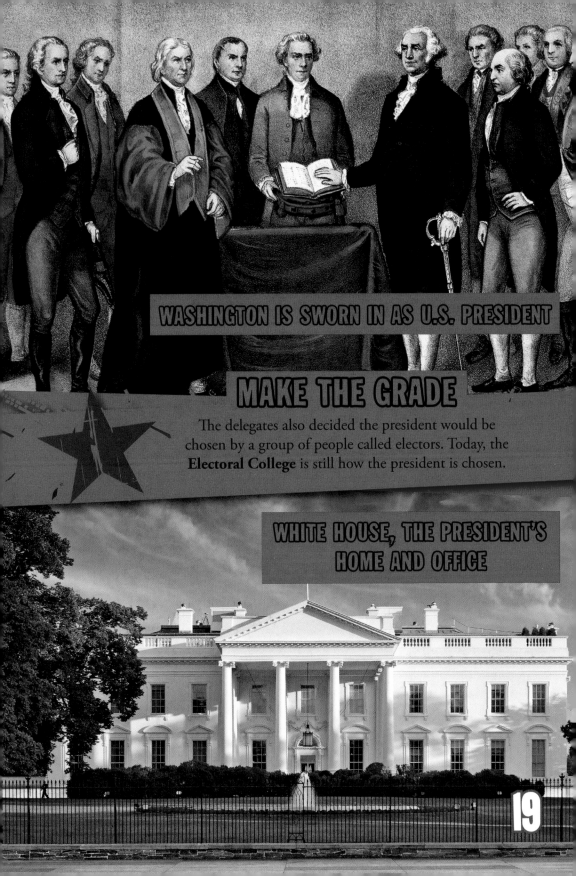

WASHINGTON IS SWORN IN AS U.S. PRESIDENT

MAKE THE GRADE

The delegates also decided the president would be chosen by a group of people called electors. Today, the **Electoral College** is still how the president is chosen.

WHITE HOUSE, THE PRESIDENT'S HOME AND OFFICE

THE JUDICIAL BRANCH

The highest court in the nation, the Supreme Court, is the top of the judicial branch. It's also included in the Constitution. The delegates decided Supreme Court judges can serve for life if they choose to, unless they do something illegal.

MAKE THE GRADE

The Supreme Court can strike down
a law that goes against the Constitution.
This power is called judicial review.

U.S. SUPREME COURT BUILDING

STATES' RIGHTS

Another **debate** at the Constitutional Convention was over states' rights. Some delegates worried the federal government under the Constitution was too strong. In fact, one part of the Constitution says federal laws are more powerful than state laws.

Many southern delegates wouldn't back the Constitution unless slavery was guarded in it. So, a part allowed enslaved people to be brought into the nation until at least 1808.

THE COMMITTEE OF DETAIL

After many details, or parts, of the Constitution had been decided, a group called the Committee of Detail got to work. This group's job was to write down the ideas of the convention as a constitution. They wrote from July 26 to August 6.

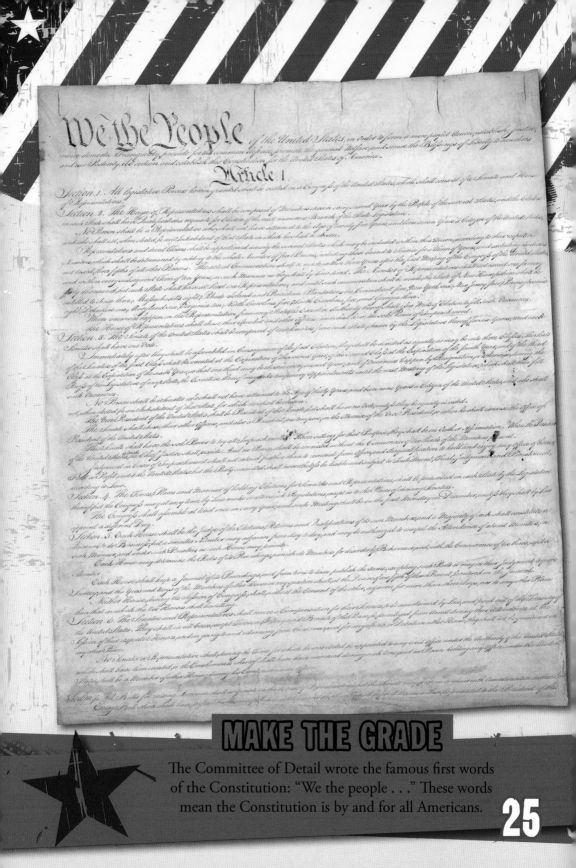

MAKE THE GRADE

The Committee of Detail wrote the famous first words of the Constitution: "We the people . . ." These words mean the Constitution is by and for all Americans.

25

THE SIGNING

The Committee of Detail presented its work to the convention on August 6. The document was debated and changed until most delegates agreed with its ideas. On September 17, 1787, 38 delegates signed the Constitution. Next, it was sent to the states.

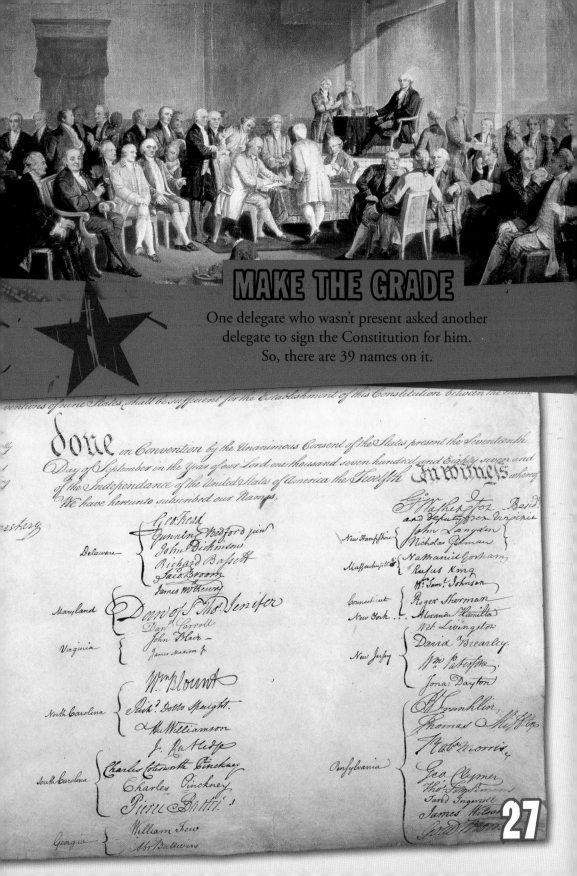

MAKE THE GRADE

One delegate who wasn't present asked another delegate to sign the Constitution for him. So, there are 39 names on it.

RATIFICATION

The Constitution says nine states had to ratify, or approve, it. However, many people wanted it to have a bill, or list, of rights to guard the rights of the states and the people. After the Constitution's supporters promised to add the Bill of Rights, the Constitution was ratified in 1788.

MAKE THE GRADE

The Constitution explains how amendments, or changes and additions, are ratified. The first 10 amendments, called the Bill of Rights (above), were ratified in 1791.

A TIMELINE OF THE U.S. CONSTITUTION

MARCH 1, 1781
The Articles of Confederation is ratified.

SEPTEMBER 3, 1783
The American Revolution ends.

AUGUST 29, 1786
Shays's Rebellion begins.

SEPTEMBER 11, 1786
The Annapolis Convention starts.

MAY 25, 1787
The Constitutional Convention begins.

MAY 29, 1787
James Madison's plan for the government is presented.

JUNE 11, 1787
The three-fifths compromise is presented.

JULY 26, 1787
The Committee of Detail begins its work.

SEPTEMBER 17, 1787
The delegates sign the U.S. Constitution.

JUNE 21, 1788
New Hampshire ratifies the Constitution, making it law.

DECEMBER 15, 1791
The Bill of Rights is ratified.

GLOSSARY

American Revolution: the war in which the colonies won their freedom from England

compromise: to reach an agreement so each side gives up something to end an argument

convention: a gathering of people who have a common interest or purpose

debate: an argument or public discussion. Also, to argue a side.

delegate: a representative of one of the 13 colonies

Electoral College: the process through which electors are chosen who then vote for the president of the United States

enslaved: being owned by another person and forced to work without pay

interstate: occurring between states

league: a group with common goals

population: the number of people who live in a place

rebellion: a fight to go against or overthrow a government

representative: one who acts for a group of people

FOR MORE INFORMATION

Books

Miloszewski, Nathan. *Federalists and Anti-Federalists*. New York, NY: PowerKids Press, 2020.

Murray, Laura K. *The U.S. Constitution*. North Mankato, MN: Capstone, 2019.

Websites

Checks and Balances
bensguide.gpo.gov/j-check-balance
Read more about the checks and balances of the U.S. government.

The Constitution
www.ducksters.com/history/us_constitution.php
Find out more about this important document.

Publisher's note to educators and parents: Our editors have carefully reviewed these websites to ensure that they are suitable for students. Many websites change frequently, however, and we cannot guarantee that a site's future contents will continue to meet our high standards of quality and educational value. Be advised that students should be closely supervised whenever they access the internet.

INDEX